Contents

C000220990

Introduction

All these cute little characters are so simple to make, by adults or children — you can make them purely for fun and place them on an iced board, or use them to decorate a cake for someone you love.

You can make your cake toppers weeks or months in advance, ready to decorate a Christmas or birthday cake. Just remember not to store them anywhere damp! Because no moulds or cutters are used, each little character you create will have its own personality and no two will be identical. You can use any modelling medium, not just sugarpaste. For example, salt dough is best for larger models and coloured modelling clay for tiny ones. Our handy templates on page 39 make it easy to judge the sizes of the various body parts of your cake toppers. The possibilities are endless. Do have a go — and be sure to have fun! We're sure you'll enjoy them.

Teddy

Everyone loves teddy bears and this little character would look great on any cake for children, whatever the occasion. Make him smooth like a new bear, or fluffy like an old, worn bear.

MATERIALS

- Sugarpaste in 'Teddy', black or brown (see page 42)
- Piece of uncooked spaghetti
- Black paste food colour and cocktail stick or toothpick
- Modelling tool

Part	Template	Color
Body	A	Teddy
Feet	2 x E	Teddy
Head	C	Teddy
Arms	2 x E	Teddy
Muzzle	G	Black or Brown
Nose	J	Black or Brown
Ears	2 x G	Teddy

See templates for sizes on page 39

1 Body Form the ball for the body into a cone shape, using 'Teddy' colour sugarpaste.

2 Feet Using one round ball of the same colour for each foot, press on to the base of the body – use a little brushed-on water to secure if necessary. Mark each foot three times along the top of the foot with the point of the tool, and once with the round end of the tool.

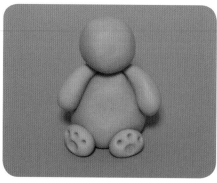

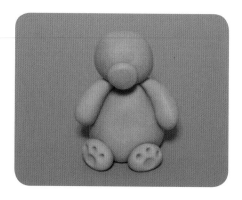

3 Arms Form a long teardrop shape for each arm (the arms should reach two thirds of the way down the body), stick each from the very top of the cone.

4 Head Push a piece of raw spaghetti down into the body and break it off ½in (12mm) above the top. Push the round head onto the protruding spaghetti, covering the top of the arms.

5 Muzzle Press a small, slightly squashed ball of icing onto the lower half of the head to form the muzzle.

6 Nose Press a tiny ball in black or brown on top of the muzzle.

7 Ears Pierce 2 x ⅛in (5mm) holes in the top of the head with pointed end of tool. Squash two balls flat and pinch one side of each to form a point. Push the point of one into a hole and repeat for the other ear. Secure with the pointed end of tool.

8 Eyes and mouth Mark eyes with black paste colour on the end of a cocktail stick (see page 46). Scribe the teddy's mouth as shown using a cocktail stick.

BLANKET
To make a blanket for your teddy, roll out 2oz (60g) of pale-coloured sugarpaste, ⅛in (2–3mm) thick, cut out a small oval, score the edges with a knife to simulate stitches and paint on little flowers or dots.

RUFFLED TEXTURE
Use a cocktail stick to scratch the surface of the teddy to make it look ruffled or fluffy.

Small Dogs

Both these dogs are made using the same technique, but look how just a few changes can make such different results! Don't forget to add a little ball for them to play with.

MATERIALS
BROWN DOG

- Chestnut brown and black sugarpaste (see page 42)
- Black paste food colour/cocktail stick or toothpick/modelling tool

Part	Template	Color
Feet	4 x F	Chestnut brown
Body	A	Chestnut brown
Head	D	Chestnut brown
Nose	H	Black
Long Ears	2 x F	Black
Tail	G	Black

MATERIALS
BROWN DOG

- White and black sugarpaste (see page 42)
- Black paste food colour/cocktail stick or toothpick/modelling tool

Part	Template	Color
Feet	4 x F	White
Body	A	White
Head	D	White
Nose	H	Black
Short Ears	2 x G	White
Tail	G	White

See templates for sizes on page 39

BROWN DOG

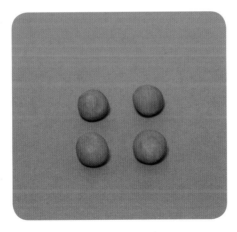

1 Feet Form four feet from round balls of sugarpaste and place in a square ¾in (19mm) apart.

2 Body Make the body into an oval shape and press it firmly down on top of the feet. Make a dent with your finger where the head is to be positioned.

3 Head Form the head into a pear shape and place – using water if necessary to stick – on to the indent.

4 Nose Mark a small hole for the mouth and above it make a deeper hole for the nose; insert a teardrop-shaped piece of black sugarpaste to form the nose.

5 Long ears Form two ears from black sugarpaste. Make two long thin cone shapes, flatten and stick one on each side of the head. Mark eyes (see page 46); add two dots above for eyebrows.

WHITE DOG

6 Tail Form a long tail shape with a point at each end, make a hole at the end of the dog's body, stick the tail in firmly and curl the end up.

7 Body and head Repeat steps 1–4 and stage 6 with the white sugarpaste, but make the head slightly more square.

8 Ears Squash two balls of sugarpaste into long ovals for the ears, flatten slightly and stick the lower third of each one to the sides of the head, securing with a little brushed-on water.

9 Short ears Bend the top part of each ear downward. Mark the eyes (see page 46) and add two tiny dots above for the eyebrows.

10 Fluffy body Use a cocktail stick to pull out the icing all over the body to create a rough fluffy look.

Penguins

These little penguins are quick and simple to make and can be placed on a Christmas cake for a lovely seasonal scene. Why not add some little white Christmas trees, too!

MATERIALS
- White, black and orange sugarpaste (see page 42)
- Black paste food colour and cocktail stick or toothpick
- Modelling tool

LARGE PENGUIN

Part	Template	Color
Body	A	White
Feet	2 x F	Orange
Beak	G	Orange

SMALL PENGUIN

Part	Template	Color
Body	D	White
Feet	2 x G	Orange
Beak	H	Orange

See templates for sizes on page 39

NOTE:
For the penguin's black back, roll out a rectangle of sugarpaste and cut a triangle 2in (5cm) at the base by about 2½in (6.5cm) high. The triangle for the smaller penguins should be about half the size of the larger one.

1 Body Form a cone from a ball of sugarpaste, with a rounded not pointed top.

2 Feet Shape each orange ball into a teardrop shape and place them next to each other in a heart shape.

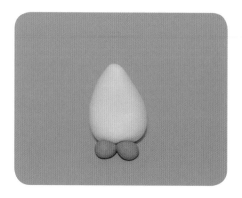

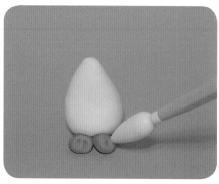

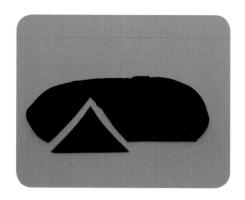

3 Add feet Place the body on the back edges of the feet and slide it toward you so that the feet become attached.

4 Mark toes Using the pointed end of the modelling tool, form three impressions on each foot to make the toes.

5 Cut triangle Roll out a small piece of black sugarpaste to a thickness of ⅛in (2–3mm), cut a triangular shape (see Note, page 8), for the penguin's back and brush the centre line with a little water.

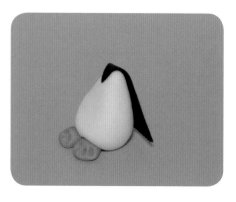

6 Stick on back Stick the black triangle to the back of the white cone with the shortest side of the triangle at the base. Bend the top of the triangle over the penguin's head.

7 Hole for beak Push a deep hole into the penguin's face just below the black point using the pointed end of the modelling tool.

8 Add beak Form a small ball of orange sugarpaste into a double pointed shape – push one end into the hole in the face. Mark the eyes (see page 46).

9 Baby penguins Make some baby penguins following exactly the same method, but with smaller balls of sugarpaste.

10 Ice From a block of white sugarpaste cut some angular pieces of icing of various sizes to create chunks of ice.

Crocodile

Why not have a go at making this unusual model?
Your snappy crocodile could be in a blue river, or climbing up
the riverbank having caught a fish for tea!

MATERIALS

- Green, white, black and light blue sugarpaste (see page 42)
- Quilting tool (pointed end)
- Modelling tool
- Black paste food colour and cocktail stick or toothpick

Part	Template	Color
Body	A + B	Green
Legs	4 x E	Green
Eye white	H	White
Eye black	J	Black
Fish body	G	Light blue
Fish tail	I	Light blue

See templates for sizes on page 39

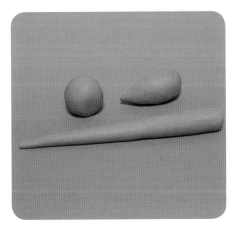

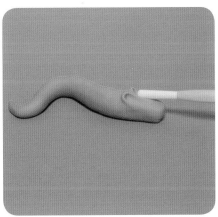

1 Body Mix balls A and B together, start to shape a cone and then elongate it until it is 7in (17.5cm) long.

2 Eye sockets Push up two big eye sockets at the thicker part of the cone, 1½in (4cm) in from the end.

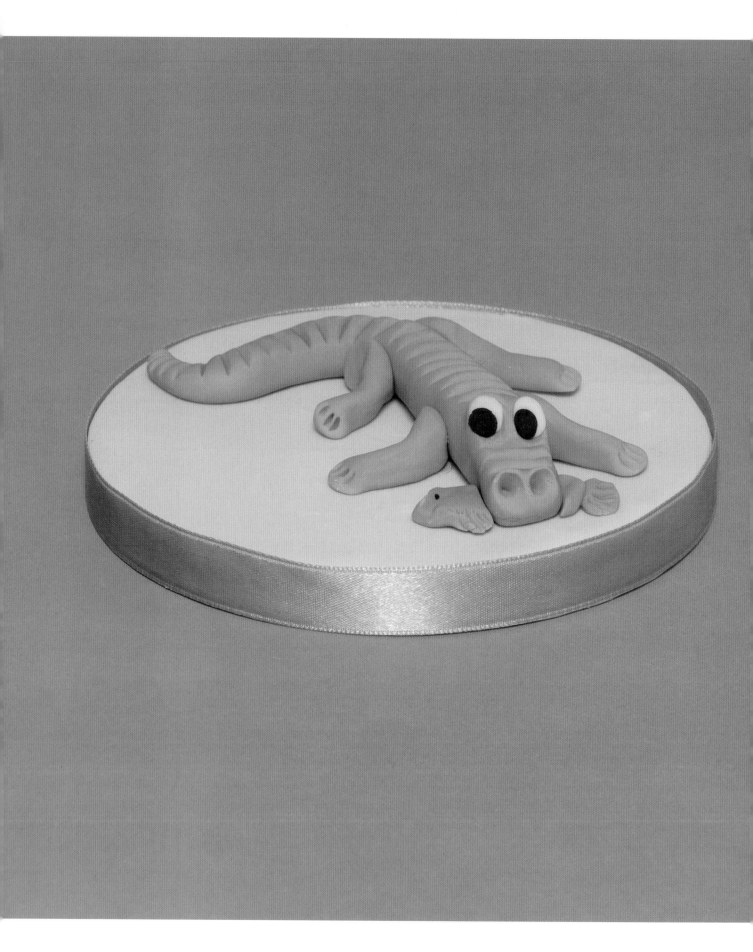

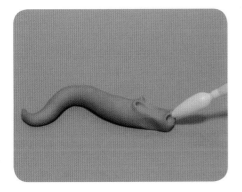

3 Nostrils Form nostrils by pushing in two smaller indentations at the end of the crocodile's face.

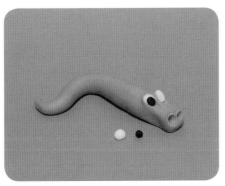

4 Eyes Add the eyes, made from a squashed ball of white with a smaller ball of black on top.

5 Ribbing Using the pointed end of the quilting tool score deep lines all the way along the nose of the crocodile and right down the back and tail.

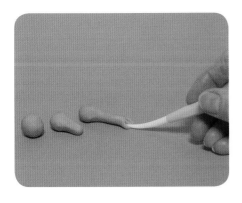

6 Legs and feet Form four fat, drumstick-shaped legs and make three impressions at the thinner end of each foot for the toes.

7 Attaching the legs Add the four legs to the body and bend them all out slightly. Stick with water if necessary.

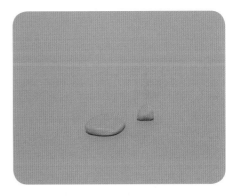

8 Fish Form the fish body and a little triangular tail.

9 Fish tail Mark the fins and tail of the fish with lines using the pointed end of the quilting tool.

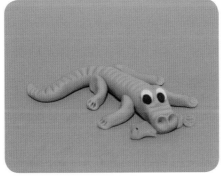

10 Hungry crocodile Cut the fish in half and place on each side of the crocodile's mouth.

Rabbits

The blue rabbit could be made in any colour you like and placed on your cake with a teddy or duck to keep him company. Your other bunny will look great in a garden scene.

MATERIALS
- Black paste food colour, cocktail stick or toothpick, piping bag (see page 47) and green royal icing (see page 48).

BLUE RABBIT
- Blue, white, brown and orange sugarpaste (see page 42).

Part	Template	Color
Body	B	Dark blue + white
Feet	2 x F	Dark blue + white
Arms	2 x E	Dark blue + white
Tummy	F	White
Head	Large D	Dark blue + white
Nose	H	Brown
Tail	E	White

BROWN RABBIT
- Brown, black, white and orange sugarpaste (see page 42).

Part	Template	Color
Body	B	Dark brown
Front legs	2 x F	Dark brown
Head	2 x E	Dark brown
Tail	F	White
Nose	Large D	Black

See templates for sizes on page 39

BLUE RABBIT

1 Body Follow steps 1–3 for Teddy (see page 2), but mix a light blue sugarpaste.

2 Tummy Squash a ball of white sugarpaste into a fat cone shape and flatten. Using a little brushed-on water to stick, press on to the rabbit's tummy.

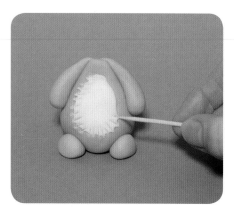

3 Fluffy tummy Use a cocktail stick to blend the edges of the white tummy into the blue.

4 Head Using light blue sugarpaste, shape the head ball into a pointed cone shape; cut through the top of the cone to form two long ears.

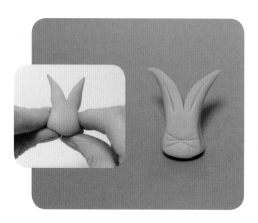

5 Ears Place your thumbs under the rabbit's head and your fingers above it; flatten the base of the head and the ears will move slightly apart (inset). Mark up each ear and the whiskers with a knife.

6 Tail and face Turn the rabbit around and place a cone-shaped tail under his bottom; score it with a cocktail stick to make it look fluffy. To complete the face, add a little brown ball for the nose insert (see Small Dogs, page 7). Mark the eyes (see page 46).

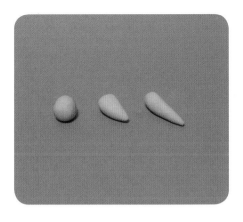

7 Carrots Form several little carrots from orange sugarpaste, mark lines on them with knife and pipe green leaves at the top – see page 48). Tuck one carrot under the rabbit's arm.

BROWN RABBIT

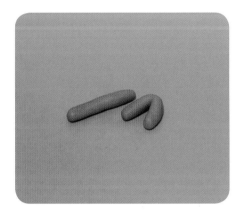

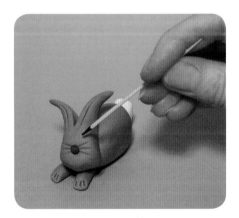

8 Front legs Roll brown sugarpaste into a sausage shape 1in (2.5cm) long, bend it into a C-shape.

9 Body and tail Make a cone-shaped body, place the tapered end over the curve of the legs. Add a fluffy tail – see stage 6.

10 Head Make the head following stages 4–6. Mark the eyes (see page 46). Score three little lines at the end of each foot for toes.

Frog

One little cheeky frog can be placed on a rock for a lovely design.
Make some extra baby frogs or, for a bit of fun, some pairs of eyes only, peeping out of the water.

MATERIALS
- Green, white, black and grey sugarpaste (see page 42)
- Piping tube
- Modelling tool

LARGE FROG

Part	Template	Color
Body	A	Green
Legs	2 x D	Green
White eye	G	White
Black eye	I	Black

SMALL FROG

Part	Template	Color
Body	C	Green
Legs	2 x E	Green
White eye	H	White
Black eye	J	Black

See templates for sizes on page 39

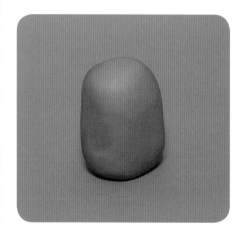

1 Body Shape the body ball into a short oval. Press it down firmly onto your work surface to flatten the base.

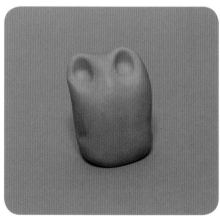

2 Face Mark indents for eyes using the rounded end of your modelling tool, pushing each indent upwards.

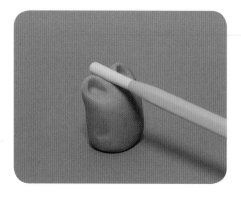

3 Face Push the rounded end of the tool down between the eye indentations.

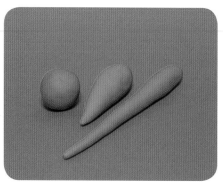

4 Legs Shape each of the leg balls into a cone and then elongate until they are 3in (7.5cm) long.

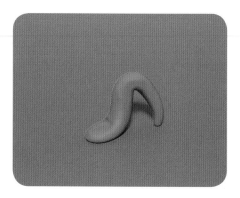

5 Leg Flatten the thickest end for the foot and bend the remaining length of the leg into an inverted V-shape.

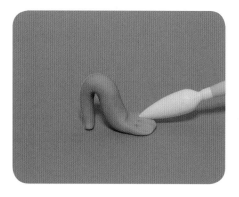

6 Toes Use the pointed end of the modelling tool to mark three impressions to create the frog's four toes.

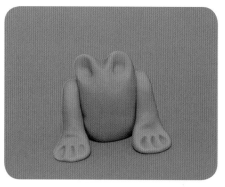

7 Add legs Stick one leg each side of the body, using a little brushed-on water to hold them firmly in place.

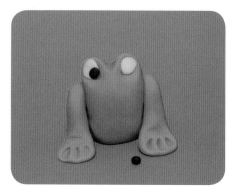

8 Eyes Squash the white balls flat and stick one in each of the eye indentations. Squash the black balls and stick on the bottom of each white ball.

9 Smile Make a smiling mouth using the large open end of a small stainless steel piping tube, press in one side firmly.

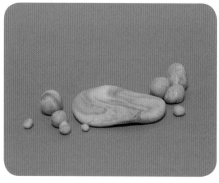

10 Rocks and pebbles Make grey sugarpaste pebbles in various shapes and sizes. Large flat ones would be suitable for your frog to sit on.

Elephant

Elephants are always a favourite model to go on a cake.
For variety, make them in different shades of pink and different sizes,
and lay some on their tummies or backs.

MATERIALS

- Sugarpaste in pink (see page 42)
- Piece of uncooked spaghetti
- Black paste food colour and cocktail stick or toothpick
- Modelling tool

Part	Template	Color
Body	A	Pink
Feet	2 x E	Pink
Arms	2 x E	Pink
Head	C	Pink
Ears	2 x E	Pink

See templates for sizes on page 39

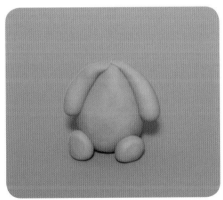

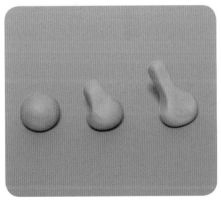

1 Body Follow stages 1–3 of Teddy (see page 2) but don't mark the toe details on each foot.

2 Head Shape the sugarpaste into a pear shape and gently pull and stretch the thinner end to form the trunk.

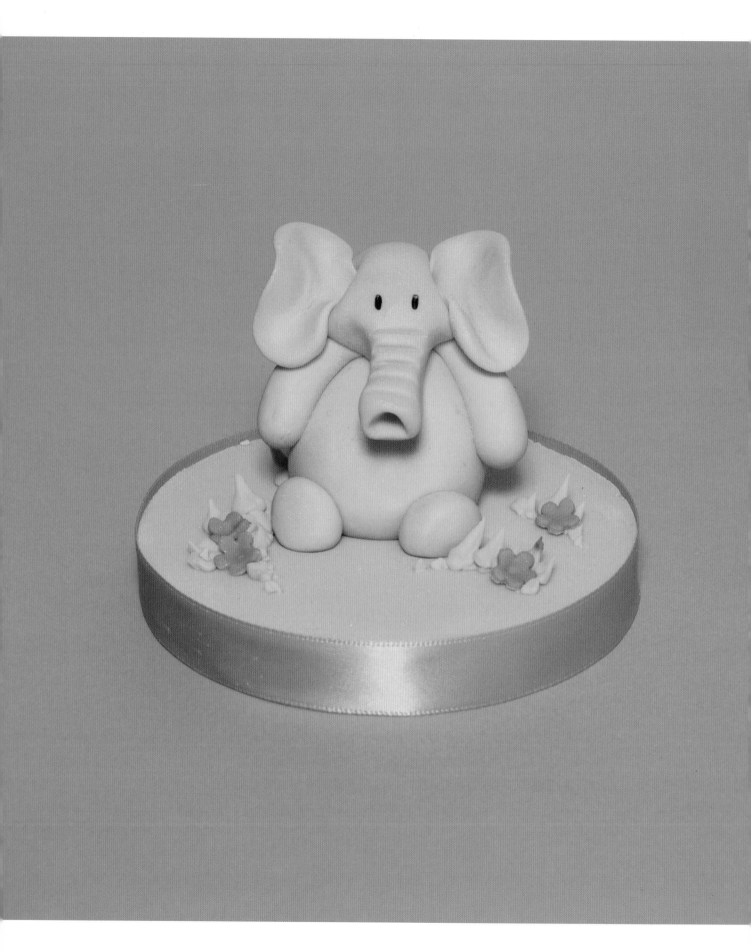

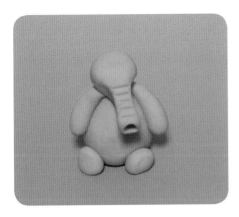

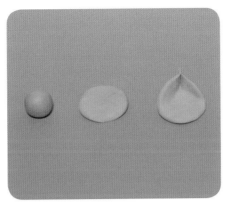

3 Trunk Push a short piece of spaghetti into the body, break it off with ⅕in (5mm) showing, and push on the head. Form a hole in the end of the trunk and score lines along its length with a knife.

4 Ears Squash each ball flat until it is ¾in (2cm) in diameter and pinch one side to form a point.

5 Earhole Make a large hole at the side of the head and push in the point of the ear, push the pointed tool in to the centre to secure. Repeat for the other ear.

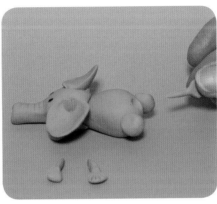

6 Ears and eyes Push the middle of the outer ear gently inwards on both sides. Mark the eyes (see page 46).

7 Tail Mark a hole in the bottom if your elephant is lying down, form a little tail and push the point in securely.

OTHER IDEAS
For an adult celebration add some little champagne bottle candles and small plastic glasses.

Cut several thin strips of tearing ribbon and curl them with the blade of a knife or scissors, arrange these around or between the elephants.

Pig

Pigs are always popular characters. Make these fat little porkers and arrange in some brown royal icing 'mud'. For a lovely farmyard scene, why not add some piglets, too?

1 Body and legs Follow stages 1–2 of Brown dog instructions (see page 5), but using pale pink sugarpaste.

2 Head Place the round ball on to the dent in the body. Press firmly to secure or use a little brushed-on water. Squash the smaller nose ball and press in on to the head.

  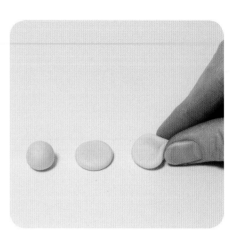

3 Nostrils Mark two holes for nostrils with the pointed end of your modelling tool.

4 Ears Make the ears (see right) and attach them to the top of the head with the points sticking upwards, then bend the point downwards.

 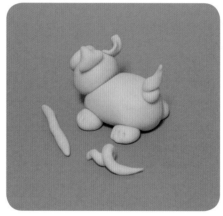

5 Eyes When both your ears are in position you can mark the eyes with black colour (see page 46). You may need to push the ears back up while marking the eyes.

6 Tail Turn your pig around and make a deep hole in the bottom. Form a long tapered sausage, push one end into the hole and twist the remaining tail into a curl.

Mouse

These little icing mice can be made in white or grey sugarpaste and, for a dinner party surprise, why not put them on your cheeseboard at the end of the meal?

MATERIALS
- Sugarpaste in grey, pink, black and yellow (see pages 42)
- Black paste food colour and cocktail stick or toothpick
- Modelling tool

Part	Template	Color
Body	A	Grey
Ears	2 x E	Grey
Inner Ear	2 x G	Pink
Nose	I	Black
Tail	E	Grey

See templates for sizes on page 39

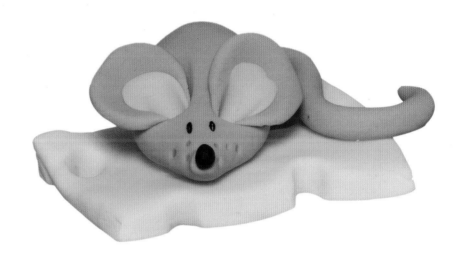

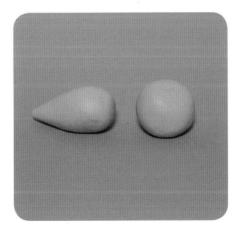

1 Body Form the round ball of grey sugarpaste into a cone shape.

2 Nose Bend the tip of the mouse's body up for the nose.

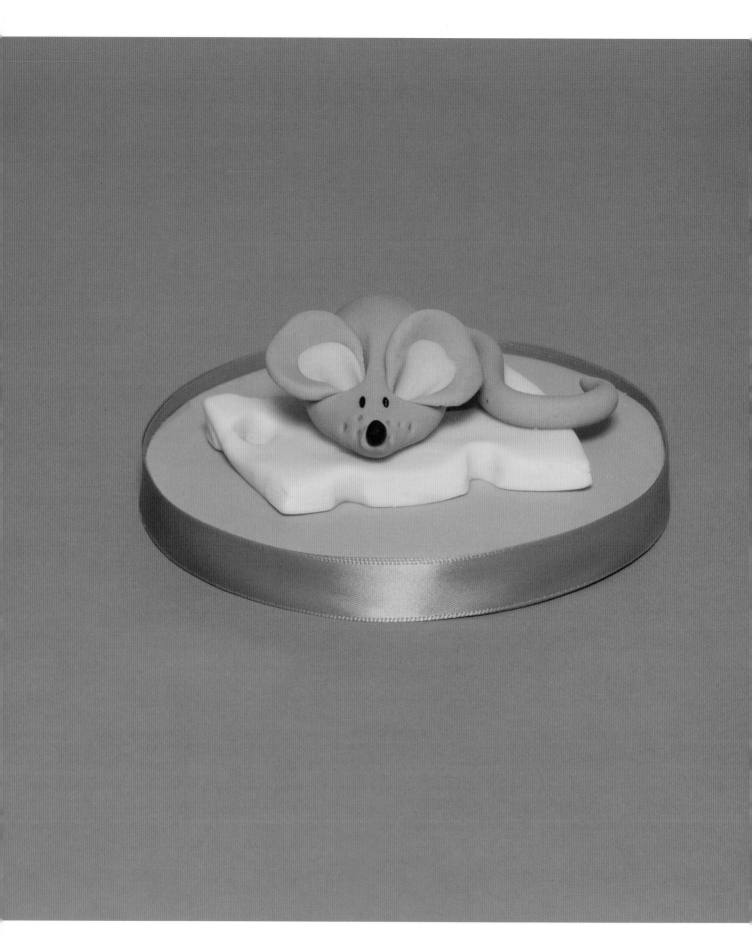

3 Ears Rest the pointed tool along the back of the mouse and push the end in to make two large holes.

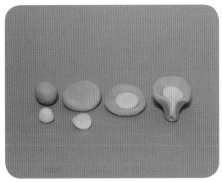

4 Squash the grey ball, press on the squashed pink ball, flatten together and then pinch one side to a point.

5 Push the point of each ear into the big holes.

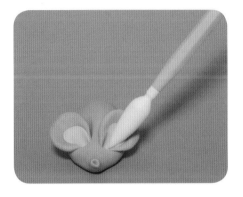

6 Push the pointed end of the tool into each ear to firmly stick it in place.

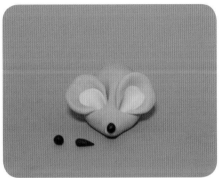

7 Nose Form a little teardrop shape from the black ball and push it into a hole in the mouse's nose.

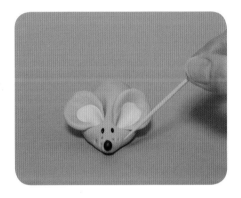

8 Eyes Mark the eyes with black paste colour (see page 46) then, with a clean cocktail stick, make little whisker holes each side of the nose.

9 Tail Form your tail into a long tapering sausage shape. Place one end under the mouse and curl the tail.

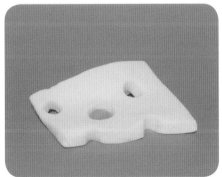

10 Cheese Roll out a very pale yellow thick wedge of sugarpaste, cut some big holes in it and push in a few indentations around the side.

Monkey

Your cheeky monkey can be part of a jungle scene.
Why not make a family group all lounging around, eating bananas and leaning on each other? Some could even be lying on their bellies or backs.

MATERIALS
- 'Teddy' brown, dark brown, white and yellow sugarpaste (see page 42)
- Modelling tool
- Black paste food colour and cocktail stick or toothpick

Part	Template	Color
Rock	A + B	Black + white (mixed)
Body	A	Teddy brown
Legs	2 x D	Teddy brown
Arms	2 x E	Teddy brown
Tail	E	Teddy brown
Head	D	Teddy brown
Nose	F	Teddy brown
Nostrils	H	Sand
Ears	2 x G	Teddy brown
Banana	F	Yellow

See templates for sizes on page 39

1 Rock and body Form a large rock shape, squash slightly. Make the body cone shaped and place on top of the rock.

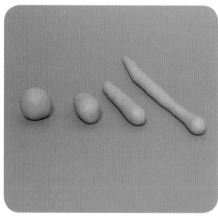

2 Arms and legs Form the legs and arms as illustrated.

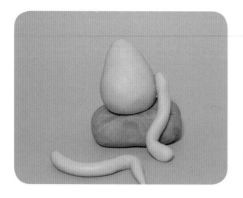

3 Legs Join the legs to the body as shown and bend the feet back. Secure with a little brushed-on water.

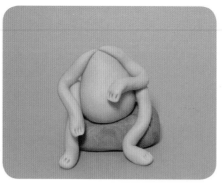

4 Arms Taper the top of the arms and stick to the shoulders. Use a cocktail stick to mark three toes at the end of each limb.

5 Head and nose Form the two balls, stick them to each other (the larger ball is the top of the head, the smaller one the nose).

6 Nostrils Squash the sand coloured sugarpaste into an oval, then flatten and press it on to the lower section of the head. Push two holes into the little nose for nostrils.

7 Head and ears Place the head on to the body with a piece of spaghetti to support it. Add the ears (see Teddy step 7, page 4). Mark the eyes (see page 46).

8 Tail Form the ball of icing for the tail into a long sausage shape. Insert one end into a hole at the back of the monkey.

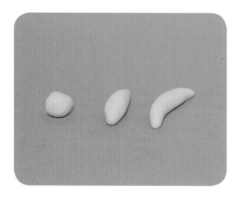

9 Banana Form a little banana from each ball of sugarpaste.

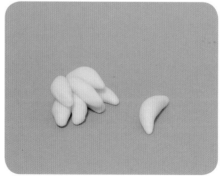

10 Bananas Place a group together to form a bunch of bananas and place one in the monkey's hand.

Ducks

This colourful little duck is the easiest character to make in the book. It would look at home in a pond scene with a group of ducklings on a blue cake and piped grass around the sides.

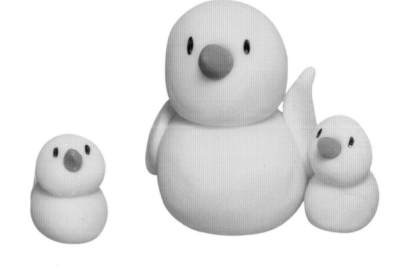

MATERIALS
- Yellow, red and brown sugarpaste (see page 42)
- Black paste food colour and cocktail stick or toothpick
- Pieces of uncooked spaghetti
- Modelling tool

LARGE DUCK

Part	Template	Color
Body	B	Yellow
Head	D	Yellow
Beak	Small G	Red
Wings	2 x F	Yellow

SMALL DUCK

Part	Template	Color
Body	E	Yellow
Head	F	Yellow
Beak	H	Red

See templates for sizes on page 39

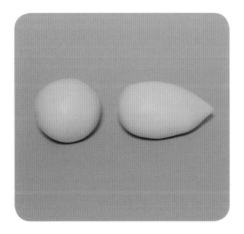
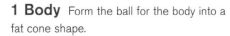

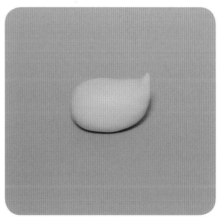

1 Body Form the ball for the body into a fat cone shape.

2 Tail Gently bend the end point upwards to form the tail.

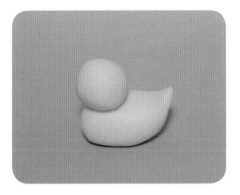

3 Head Stick the round ball for the head on to the fat end of the cone, using a little brushed-on water to secure if necessary.

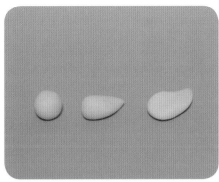

4 Wings Make two small balls, form each one into a teardrop shape, then bend the point upwards and flatten each one.

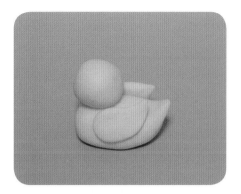

5 Join wings Using a little brushed-on water to secure, stick one wing to each side of the body.

6 Beak Form the red ball for the beak into a long diamond shape, then make hole in the face and push in one point firmly.

7 Eyes Add long eyes to the duck, marked with black paste colour on the end of a cocktail stick (see page 46).

8 Baby ducks Make a few baby ducks ready to go on your 'pond' – there is no need to add wings to the baby ducks.

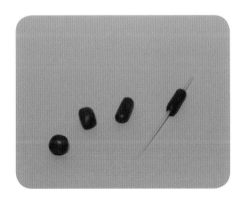

9 Bulrushes Roll some small pieces of brown sugarpaste into a cylinder shape, push short lengths of raw spaghetti into each one – ensure the spaghetti is different lengths.

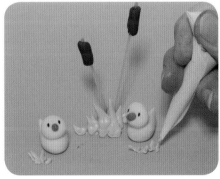

10 Grass Following instructions for piping hair and grass on page 48, pipe green grass spikes around the base of the bulrushes.

Tiger

This lovely lazy tiger is having a rest on a log.
You could also surround him with lots of bright green piped grass
and place him directly on your cake, as if he's hiding in a jungle.

MATERIALS

- Orange, white, black and dark brown sugarpaste (see page 42)
- Modelling tool
- Black paste food colour and cocktail stick or toothpick
- Fine paintbrush

Part	Template	Color
Body	A	Orange
Legs	4 x E	Orange
Head	D	Orange
Tail	F	Orange
Nose	F	White
Nose tip	H	Black
Ears	Small G x 2	Orange
Tree trunk	A + B	Dark brown

See templates for sizes on page 39

NOTE:

If you wish your tiger to lie on the tree trunk, follow steps 9 and 10 first, then make the model on top.

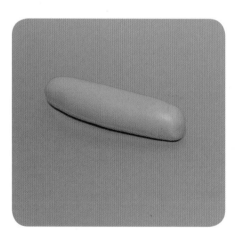
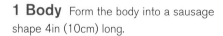

1 Body Form the body into a sausage shape 4in (10cm) long.

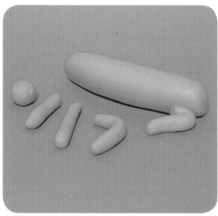

2 Legs Roll each leg into a sausage shape 1½in (4cm) long; bend each into a V-shape and stick one leg to each corner of the body.

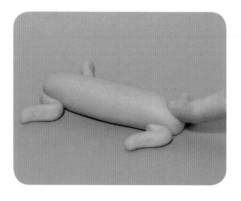

3 Neck Use your finger to make a dent at the neck of the tiger. This will enable his head to face upwards.

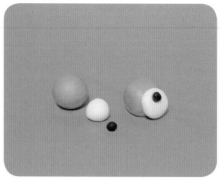

4 Head Form the three balls of icing, join the orange and white balls, squash together to stick, make a hole at the top of the white ball and insert a black teardrop-shaped nose-tip.

5 Ears Follow instructions for Teddy ears, step 7 (page 4), to complete the head.

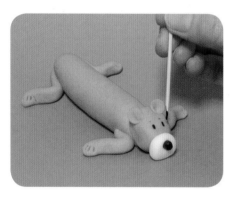

6 Eyes and toes Add eyes to the head (see page 46). Mark three toes at the end of each foot.

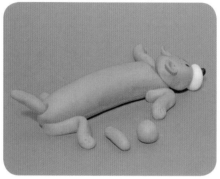

7 Tail Form a 1½in (4cm) long tail. Make a deep hole in the bottom of the tiger and push the tail in firmly.

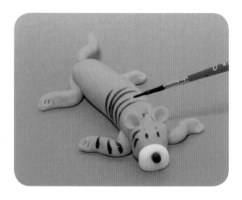

8 Stripes Dilute your black paste colour with a little water and, using a fine-quality brush, paint the stripes all over the tiger, from the bottom upwards.

9 Tree trunk Form a large flat sausage shape – cut one end straight and the other end so that it slopes downwards.

10 Branches Cut a few little branches and scratch the surface of the 'bark' roughly.

Techniques

SUGARPASTE TEMPLATES

If you are a beginner, practise making a duck and teddy before you make one of the more complicated models. Always use the templates below for all your animals, as this will save you having to guess the size of each body part.

All the models in this book have been made with bought sugarpaste/rolled fondant icing. I have used Regalice throughout. If you use a different brand, ensure that it isn't too sticky or too elastic in texture.

METHOD
Each time you create a part of your model, roll it into a smooth ball in the palms of your hands. The warmth of your hands will soften the paste and remove any lines or cracks from its surface. Now match the ball to the correct size ball on the chart.

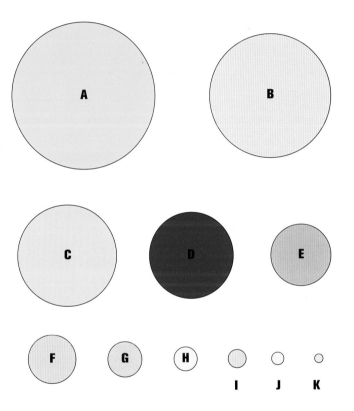

TIP
If your instructions say to use a 'Small A' size, form a ball that fits well inside the outline. Alternatively a 'Large B' would cover the outer rim of the circle.

Equipment for models

Only a few basic tools are required to create the characters in this book and they can all be bought from your local sugarcraft supplier.

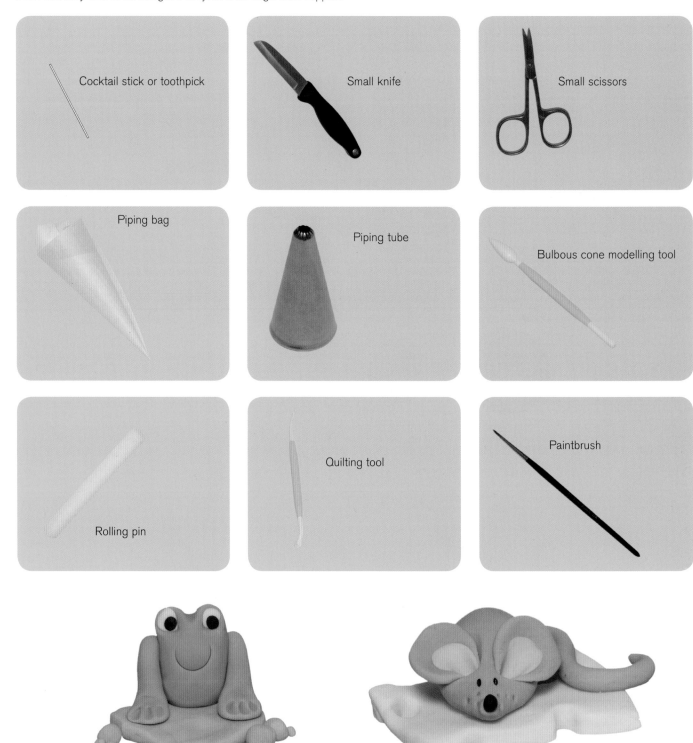

Cocktail stick or toothpick

Small knife

Small scissors

Piping bag

Piping tube

Bulbous cone modelling tool

Rolling pin

Quilting tool

Paintbrush

Ingredients for models

All of these ingredients can be bought in advance and stored ready-to-use, apart from royal icing, which needs to be made up freshly when required and stored in an airtight bag.

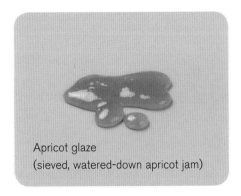

Apricot glaze
(sieved, watered-down apricot jam)

Paste food colours

Icing sugar

Coloured sugarpaste/rolled fondant

White sugarpaste/rolled fondant

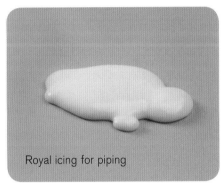

Royal icing for piping

Spaghetti

Sugarpaste

This is sometimes referred to as 'fondant' or 'roll-out' icing. It is easily bought in sugarcraft shops and supermarkets, and is available in white and many different colours. Using ready-coloured paste can save a lot of time, especially with darker colours such as red, green or black.

COLOURING SUGARPASTE/ ROYAL ICING

If you cannot buy readymade sugarpaste in the colour you require, buy white sugarpaste and colour it yourself. Use paste colours for best results as they are more concentrated and give deeper, richer colours. Royal icing is coloured in the same way.

1 Make a hole with your thumb in the middle of the piece of paste to be coloured. Dip a cocktail stick or toothpick into your chosen colour, then transfer the colour into the hole.

2 Fold the paste over and start to knead the colour in, using icing (confectioner's) sugar to prevent it sticking to the work surface or to your hands. Add more colour as necessary to achieve the colour you require, but take care not to add too much.

TIP

If you wish to colour your own sugarpaste icing, use paste colours in preference to powder or liquid colours. Powder colours can create a grainy effect and liquid colours can change the consistency of your sugarpaste and make it sticky.

BASIC COLOURS

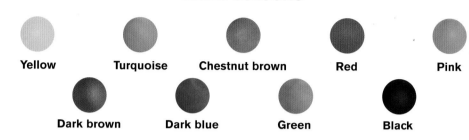

Yellow   Turquoise   Chestnut brown   Red   Pink

Dark brown   Dark blue   Green   Black

MIXED COLOURS

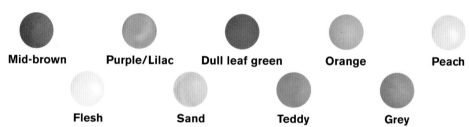

Mid-brown   Purple/Lilac   Dull leaf green   Orange   Peach

Flesh   Sand   Teddy   Grey

To achieve	Mix
Mid-brown	Chestnut brown and dark brown
Orange	Yellow and red
Sand	Orange, yellow and brown + lots of white sugarpaste
Purple/lilac	Pink and blue
Peach	Pink and yellow + white sugarpaste
Teddy'	Orange and brown + white sugarpaste
Dull leaf green	Pink and yellow (tiny amounts of each) + lots of white sugarpaste
Flesh	Pink and yellow (tiny amounts of each) + lots of white sugarpaste
Grey	Tiny amount of black mixed with white sugarpaste

Covering a cake and board

Always place your cake on a board at least 2in (5cm) larger than the cake. If you use a much larger board, you can position some models down on to the board too, for a more effective finished design.

1 Sandwich your cake with the filling of your choice, then spread thinly all over with butter cream.

2 Roll out the sugarpaste to a thickness of ⅛in (3mm) on a surface dusted with icing sugar. Bring your cake as near to the rolled-out icing as possible, wrap the icing over your rolling pin, and gently place it on the cake.

3 Gently smooth the icing around the top edge of the cake using the palms of your hands.

4 Work your way smoothly down the sides of the cake until you reach the base.

5 Use a smoother in circular motions to gently 'polish' the top of the cake, flatten the top and create a sheen on the surface of your icing.

6 Using small cuts, trim the icing off around the bottom of your cake.

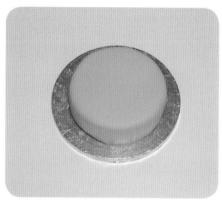

7 Use the smoother around the sides of the cake to create beautifully straight sides.

8 Your cake is now ready to finish. To cover the silver board edge, follow the next four stages.

9 Brush on a very thin layer of water or apricot glaze.

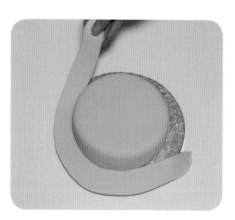

10 Roll out a strip of sugarpaste. Cut a straight edge on one side and wrap it around the silver board, adding additional strips until the board edge is covered.

11 Trim all around the edge with small cuts; wipe your knife frequently and continue until the icing is trimmed all the way round.

12 Smooth around the icing on the board, especially over the joins.

Covering a cake drum/board

Placing your models on a ready-iced cake drum or board is a brilliant idea if you want to keep them after the cake has been cut and eaten. If you use a thick drum cover the edge with a co-ordinating ribbon.

YOU WILL NEED

- Cake drum
- Pastry brush
- Apricot glaze (see page 41)
- Sugarpaste (see page 42)

1 Thinly brush the top of your board or cake drum with apricot glaze.

2 Roll out your piece of sugarpaste to a ⅛in (3mm) thickness, place over your board and roll over with a rolling pin.

3 Trim around the edge with small cuts, cleaning the blade of your knife frequently.

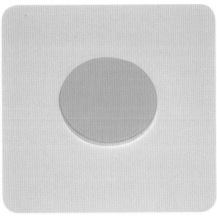

4 Your iced board is now ready to decorate.

How to mark eyes

Dip the end of your cocktail stick (or toothpick) into black paste colour and, following the instructions below, mark the eyes.

YOU WILL NEED
- Cocktail stick or toothpick
- Black paste colour

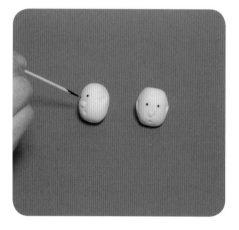

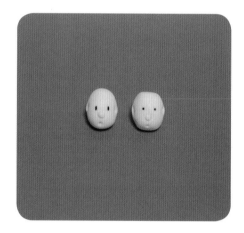

Do not mark the eyes as dots
Never push a cocktail stick or toothpick into the front of the face as this will form a little round eye and your model will look mean or unfriendly.

Mark oval or long eyes
Rest the black tip of the cocktail stick against the face to mark the eyes, approaching the head at the angle shown in the picture to ensure that the eyes are long, rather than round dots.

Compare the two faces
The one with long eyes (left) is much more friendly and appealing than the one with dot eyes (right).

Making a piping bag

YOU WILL NEED

• Greaseproof or silicone paper

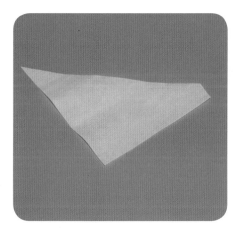

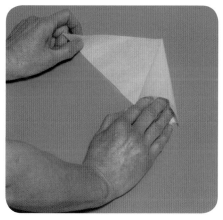

1 Cut a piece of greaseproof or silicone paper into a long triangle with one corner cut off. If right-handed, have this corner on your right, if left-handed have it on your left.

2 Pick up the right hand corner and twist it inwards until a tight point is formed in the middle of the long side.

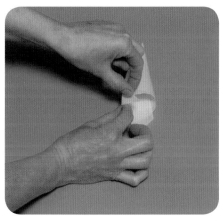

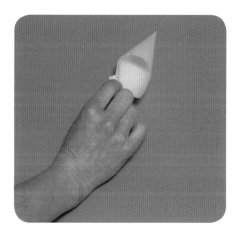

3 Rotate your hand inside until you have rolled to the end of the triangle and your cone is complete.

4 Bend the point of the paper inwards and tuck firmly into the cone.

5 Make a little rip halfway along, then fold over and bend one side inwards – this will secure the bag and stop it unravelling when you let go of it.

Making royal icing for piping

Royal icing is used for piping hair and piping grass, and it's also great for making little snowy patches on your Christmas scenes, or sticking your models to your cake.

YOU WILL NEED

- 3 fl oz (90ml) albumen solution (reconstituted egg white)
- 1lb/3 cups (500g) icing sugar, sifted
- 1 teaspoon glycerine
- Colouring (if required – see page 42)

Put all the ingredients together in a bowl and beat with an electric mixer on slow speed until peaked consistency is achieved.

TIP
When storing royal icing, always cover it with a damp cloth, or put in a sealed container to prevent it drying out.

Piping hair and grass

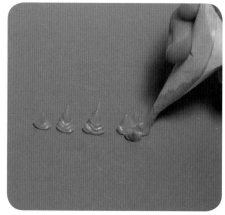

1 Colour your royal icing and fill one third of your piping bag. Fold the open end of the bag over several times, flatten the pointed end, then cut the end as shown.

2 Gently squeeze a blob of icing out of the bag, stop squeezing and pull away and you will have formed a little spike of grass or hair.